Totems & More!
A Kid's Guide To Ketchikan, Alaska

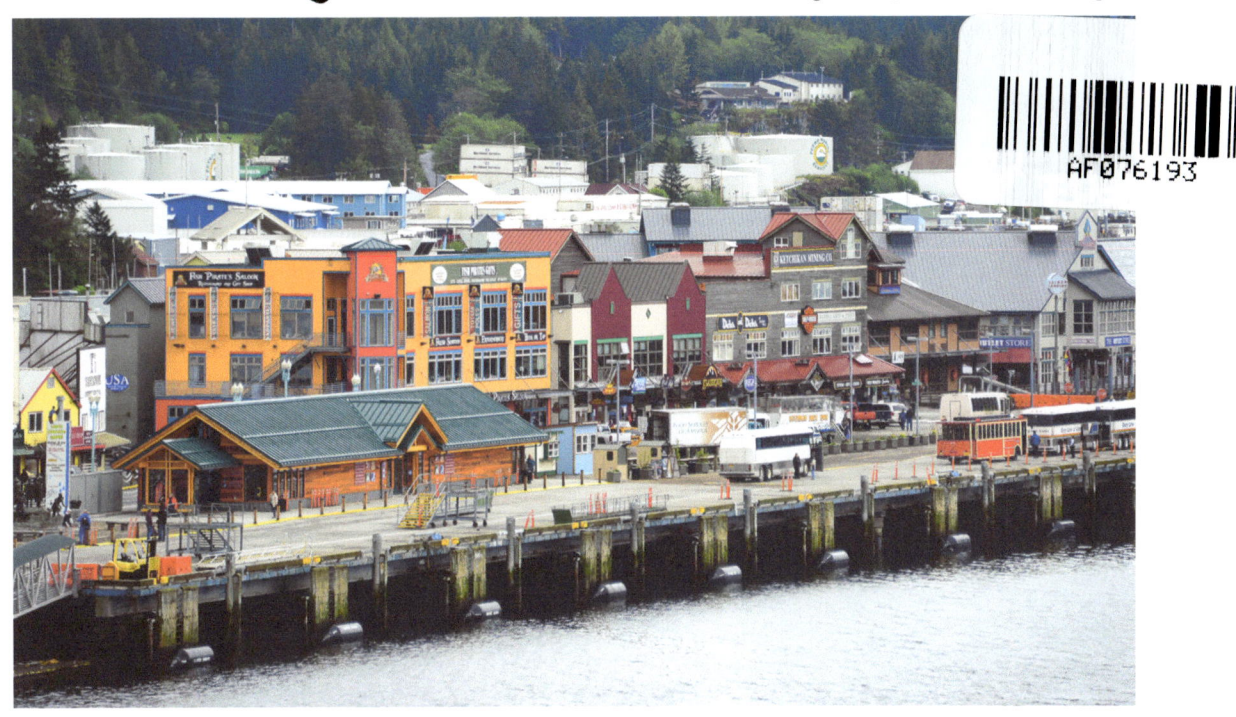

Photography by John D. Weigand
Poetry by Penelope Dyan

Bellissima Publishing, LLC
Jamul, California
www.bellissimapublishing.com

Copyright © 2013 by Penny D. Weigand and John D. Weigand

All rights reserved. No part of this book may be
reproduced or transmitted in any form or by any means,
electronic or mechanical, including photocopying,
recording, or by any other means, or by any information or
storage retrieval system, without permission from the publisher.

ISBN 978-1-61477-107-4
First Edition

Ancient Indian Proverb

Treat the earth well.
It was not given to you by your parents,
it was loaned to you by your children.
We do not inherit the Earth from our Ancestors,
we borrow it from our Children

Totems & More!
Bellissima Publishing, LLC

Introduction

Ketchikan, Alaska is the fifth most populous city in the state of Alaska with a population of only 8050 as of 2010. Ketchikan is a small town with a big heart and a dedication to preserving its very unique past. An entire museum, the Totem Heritage Center, is devoted to the story of totem poles, explaining the importance these works of art have and continue to have on the native people of Alaska. And as you will learn at the museum, totem poles were placed outside homes, and in some places still are placed outside homes, to tell the story of the people and their ancestors. It was one way ancient peoples communicated with one another and left their history behind, much like a scribe, for those you would come after them. Ketchikan is named after the Ketchikan Creek that flows through the town. And as you will see in this book there is a shopping place called Creek Street that not only has historical significance of a somewhat sordid nature, but it is also built right over Ketchikan Creek, an old historical area preserved for us to enjoy. Written by the award winning author, attorney and former teacher, Penelope Dyan, with photography by John D. Weigand, this book is sure to delight any child as he or she practices reading skills through word recognition, repetition and rhyme. There is also a Bellissimavideo music video on YouTube that goes along with this book to make learning even more fun!

Totems & More!
Bellissima Publishing, LLC

Totems & More!
A Kid's Guide To Ketchikan, Alaska

Photography by John D. Weigand
Poetry by Penelope Dyan

From out of the melting glaciers,
blue with time and cold,
there is a story waiting to be heard,
a story waiting to be told.

Each person walks a path
in his or her life,
that is full of tenderness and love,
and full of wonder and strife.

And here is one thing
that you should know.
You need to take the time
to watch the flowers grow.

As the icy Glaciers
melt and change,
and as you witness all the majesty,
you remember
the connections and circle of life,
and you think about
how things are supposed
to remain and be!

And then you laugh and you smile,
because this is NOT a crocodile,
or a Tyrannosaurus Rex Totem.
You are told that it's a bear!
It is weathered with time.
It has NO ears OR carved hair.

And you take a long look at this
wonderful, wonderful face!
It is carved into the totem,
on the pole, in its sacred place.
It is here to tell you
a very special story
about a family's life heritage,
about a family's days of glory.

Then after looking at the totems,
when you are all done,
you go outside
the Totem Heritage Center,
to picnic and to have some fun.
There you see a babbling creek
between some trees
through which you peek.

Later, you see a flag,
the old red, white and blue!
You decide that this means
something important to you.
Your mother tells you Alaska
became state number 49
on January 3, 1959.
And so you give a little salute,
and your mother exclaims,
"That's really cute!"

Then mom decides
the talking should stop.
And she walks right into
a duty free shop!
Dad looks at her and says,
"Please honey . . .
Try not to spend too much money."

The shopping area in which you walk
(with water beneath your feet)
is colorful; and it goes by the
name of 'Creek Street.'
You and Dad stop and eat
(from a snack wagon)
a hot dog or two,
because what else
should a kid and a dad
like you do?

As you leave,
you notice all the
color of this small town,
as you see the houses nestled
upon the rain soaked ground.
The rain falls gently
upon your head,
and there is no other place
you'd rather be instead.

So you sadly turn,
and you walk away,
on this not so blustery day.
Then the rain ever so softly
falls down to the ground,
glistening the walkway,
not making a sound.

*"Be still, sad heart, and cease repining;
Behind the clouds is the sun still shining;
Thy fate is the common fate of all,
Into each life some rain must fall..."*

HENRY WADSWORTH LONGFELLOW

www.ingramcontent.com/pod-product-compliance
Ingram Content Group UK Ltd.
Pitfield, Milton Keynes, MK11 3LW, UK
UKHW060135240426
12048UKWH00002B/48